My Name is Emily I Am Ten and I Have Asperger's Syndrome
(An Autobiography typed by my mom)

My name is Emily Margaret, and I am ten years old. I have what is called Asperger's Syndrome. It is a form of Autism. My mother tells me that it's just a little harder for me to understand certain things, I guess that's okay. She tells me that when I was a baby it took me a little longer to crawl, and walk, but she said that's okay because I can do those things now if I want. I don't really crawl anymore, that is for babies unless you are playing hide and go seek under the bed then I guess it's okay. My mom says this book is a little all over the place, but you have to understand people with Asperger's to know that's how we talk.

1

My Sister

  I have an older sister her name is Madilyn she's not nice all the time, she is a teenager and it's a law that says teenagers need to be mean. That's what my mother told me, but when I'm a teenager my mother said that I don't have to follow that law. I don't really ever get mad that is because I don't really feel that emotion too much because of my Asperger's some Asperger's kids feel it too much. I know my sister loves me even though she doesn't tell me all the time. I tend to feel sad a lot and I don't make a sound this is what mom calls shut down. Shut down is when I cry with no sound and don't look at people. When this happens my whole day is done. It usually happens when I have stress like the first day of school, or when I forget my homework (I usually have people helping me with packing my homework, cause I am what you call disorganized). I do not like bad grades they make me shut down to. Mom says being disorganized is part of who I am, and that is why sometimes it's good to have someone help you with that, like your own secretary. I have lots of other people that help me too, my social worker helps me to work on shut down, and to tell her when other kids hurt me. I don't always tell on friends cause then they won't be my friend anymore. The social worker tells me that's not true, and if they hurt me they weren't really my friend to begin with.   I try to make friends, but it is not always easy with my Asperger's I like to play with my friend, but sometimes I like to play alone and just have my friends close by. They don't always understand I'm not ignoring them, I just want to play my own games.

Me and My Sister Madilyn

Noises and Sleepovers

I can' t do sleepovers either I like to know where everything is, and other people put things where ever they want so I feel more comfortable at home. Sometimes other people's family members talk too loud to. I use to really be afraid of loud noises, I would hold my ears and hide. Once when we went on a field trip for school we went to this museum to see King Tut, I like mummies and I could tell you a bunch more about mummies and Egypt, but I need to talk about noise. We were eating lunch in the room and too many people were talking at the same time so I had to hide under the table until we were done with lunch. Too many people talking loud at the same time was hard for me, mom calls it sensory overload. That means too many things are going on at one time for me to figure out. Loud noises are still hard sometimes, oh and squeaky noises to. I have tried to teach my self to ignore the noises and shut them out so I can only hear myself talking in my head. Sometimes that is really hard, but I want to eat lunch with my friends. For a long time I had to eat in the office with the secretary, she was nice, but she didn't like the things that my friends do. I try very hard to make myself do things that scare me, mom helps we talk about them a lot before I do them. Sometimes we talk about them for a couple days. Like when I first stayed over at my best friend Kate's. I was really scared because their things weren't my things, and what if I needed my things they wouldn't be there. My mom told me that I would have lots of fun because Kate understands me, and she lets me have my space. I got pretty far into our sleepover, but I had to have my Aunt Pattii pick me up she lives two doors down. She has some of my stuff at her house so it makes me feel safe.

Grandma Peg

My grandma Peg use to live there, she was my closest person, we did everything together. We would color, sing, and go shopping with a list. I loved to make the list we needed one every time we would shop so we don't forget anything. Grandma helped me with my homework, and we watched our favorite shows. My mom would go to work and my dad would pick me up, but in between grandma and I would make cookies and sing Winnie the Pooh songs. I really love Winnie the Pooh, I think it's because it's quiet, I could watch it all day but no one will let me. They say they can't stand to watch it anymore. I get to watch it on my TV in my room. Grandma and I would read a lot we had a bunch of books, actually she would read to me I was to little at the time. Aunt Patti is a teacher that teaches library and computer so she has a million books at the house. One day my grandma got the cancer, that is the worse kind of disease you can get, she died. I didn't want to talk about it for at least one year. I miss my grandma, and now I can talk about her sometimes.

Grandma Peg and Aunt Pattii

<u>*Camping*</u>

I keep trying the sleepover, and I can stay over by two peoples' houses now Kate and my friend Katherine. Katherine's mom is my girl scout leader, my mom puts me in a lot of activities so I can make friends. I like girl scouts they don't make me feel like I'm different. They help everyone, we make things and do a bunch of good things for others. We have camp outs, my first camp out was really scarey, but when I was in brownies that is before you become a girl scout, Kate's mom was the leader and we went on a camp out. I didn't stay my mom came and brought me home. She brought my stuff in case I wanted to stay, but I couldn't, Kate's mom said that was okay and we could try it again. This time I was in Katherine's mom's troop, I got to call my mom about five times. The only hard part was when it got dark, but I got through it, everyone helped me. Now it's not so bad but, I still call my mom. I'm also in ice skating, my sister is an ice skater too. I always watched her skate and I wanted to try so my mom said I could. I have a hard time paying too much attention, but I can do the moves. It just takes me a little longer to learn them. I am on the syncro team, we all skate together and do the same moves. I like this better because it's like being in a straight line and not one thing is out of place. There are certain things I have to have the way I want them, like I line up all my small toys when I play with them. My stuffed animals all have to be dressed, and I like to watch funny videos on my computer. I think I like that because my friends like to watch them. This way we have something in common.

Katherine and me

Scare Things

I like scarey things, even though I can't go into a Halloween store, it scares me too much. Every Halloween my dad tries to get me to go in, we stand and stare in, but I can't make my feet move. This year I think try again. Halloween is my favorite holiday, I love the candy and trick or treating with my friend Kate. We always go around her block because grandma would take me there, and it's round no walking in straight lines. We get a lot of candy and soda, then we eat pizza, I think it's the best part of Halloween. After that dad takes me to the neighbors next door to our house just so we can spend time together, it's his favorite holiday to. We both can't wait to decorate the house, dad buys real creepy stuff, but I don't look when we decorate, I close my eyes. If there is something too creepy I walk around the other way. I usually decorate the inside, it's not creepy in there. I know that in Mexico the people have a day to remember their dead, and maybe someday I will go there and remember grandma, but I think she goes trick or treating at the place she went to. Aunt Patti is my best friend we do things together like make decoration for the holidays, bake cookies, and watch movies. Sometimes we have sleepovers, like I said I have stuff there so I'm okay most of the time, sometime I have to call my mom to see if she misses me, and my stuff is okay.

It is Fun to Dress Up

Michigan

Aunt Pattii took care of me to when my mom had her surgery, she took us to Michigan we got to go on a boat, my uncle Mike showed me the right way to get on the boat so I told everyone how to get on the boat the right way. Then we did this thing called tubing, nobody told me really what that was. It is this big inner tube that is tied on to the boat and it pulls you around. Aunt Pattii asked me if I wanted to go first I said okay they put me in the tube, I wasn't so sure about it but I kept quiet. I wasn't afraid of the water cause I taught myself to swim on my back. Mom was really impressed, because I was only six. Uncle Mike started the boat and it pulled me, I was on my belly it kind of hurt when he would hit the bumpy waves. He didn't go too fast and I held on for a while then I slide off the tube. It was Madilyn's turn next she sat down on the tube and bounced all over, I think uncle Mike went faster for her. Aunt Pattii and I laughed as we watched her bounce. I like Michigan you can find a lot of bugs and snails there. I like bugs and snails they are fascinating to me. I look for them under rocks and under the pier. My mom, dad, and Madilyn took a trip to Michigan last summer we went to

Frankenmuth, it's a German town in Michigan. They had fun things to do and see, they have a Christmas store that is open all year with lots of light and ornaments. We had fun looking at all that stuff. They had three pools in the hotel we stayed at, and a game room. I like the hot tub I go in there and talk to people my mom says that some people are there to relax and they don't want you to talk to them. I know sometimes I talk too much and my mom tells me her ears need a break and that we can talk more about stuff later. I guess all peoples' ears need a break, because sometimes they stop listening. Mom says that is only because I am giving them too much information, and they can't keep it all in their heads like I can. I love to travel with my family, I wish we could go on more trips, but mom says we can't afford them. My mom had to stop working to take care of grandma, and now she can't work because she needs to help me. She says I'm more important right now, and that someday when I can manage on my own she can go back to work and we will travel more. I hope that will be soon. We work on a lot of things, my mom and I she says autism is an in your face disease.

My Tutor Kevin

You can't let up on things, that is why we have Kevin, he is my advocate and tutor, he helps me too. This gives mom a little break, sometimes homework is hard and I get too much. Kevin talks to the teachers and tells them how they can help me learn better. Then they help me organize and help me with the important stuff, and not the stuff called busy work. I guess busy work is what they give the kids without autism, this keeps them in the house after school so they can't go to the park. Kevin teaches me how to write stories and about adding information. Writing is hard and long, but I'm learning to deal with it. Math is hard for me Kevin tells mom it's because it's not a visual thing if I could find away to see it like a story with pictures then it would be easier, but do you see a math story? I'm sure they have books like that, but I still reading **Super Fudge,** by Judy Blume.

I Like Books and Science

 I like to know the authors of all the stories I read. Mom had me take an after school class on authors at our school, when I was in first grade we learned about Tommy De Paolo, and Marc Brown he writes Arthur books, grandma and I loved to watch Arthur. Kevin and I talk about social studies he knows all about the different Indians like Aztec, Inca, and Anasazi. I remember a lot about the information we talk about. It's like my mind is a book and it stores stuff up there. I'm good at remembering things so mom tells me stuff to remember because she knows I will. School is fun I like my teachers my best subject is science I think it's because it's interesting, and they study bugs and stuff. I like doing experiments and I can remember how to do things in order. Tests can be hard, but sometimes the teachers can read them to me, and I can answer them with my words instead of writing them down. It takes a long time to write them down. I have a computer now called a NEO I don't know what that stands for, but my mom says it's like a typewriter, you can only see two sentences at a time. She likes the laptop better, but we can't take that to school. I can do my projects on the laptop though, it's fun I get to change the color of the letters sometimes. I don't type real fast, but if I practice someday I will.

Things That Bother Me

I have problems with certain things, I wash my hands a lot so I don't get germs, germs make you sick and some germs make you die. My mom says that is over dramatic, but I do need to wash my hands maybe not so much. I tried using hand sanitizer, but it dried out my hands too much and they cracked. My mom said germs would get into the cracks so we needed to moisturize them with lotion. She bought me some antibacterial lotion now, and my hands don't crack. I can't wear certain colors like yellow, I don't like yellow it's too bright. I don't like some reds and poopy color green. Once my dad wanted to wear a poopy color green shirt I had to make him change or I wouldn't go out with him. He changed it he really wanted to get out of the house so he didn't argue. I don't like socks with bumpy lines in the toe, or shirts with collars. I don't like shirts that button either, I like buttons but only on the finger puppets I make for my friends. I don't like anything zipped up higher than two inched above my belly button, if it's to high I just unzip it. Mom likes my jackets zipped higher in the winter, but I don't so she wraps a scarf around my neck and tucks it into my jacket. When she isn't looking I take it off. I need to take off my shoes and socks as soon as I get home from school, I like my feet to be bare.

My Calming Things

I also have a yoga ball I sit on it helps me to calm down and stay in one place. I love my yoga ball, but it gets in the way when people walk through the house. At school I use to sit on a bumpy cushion to keep me focused in class, I got too big for the bumpy cushion now. They try a lot of different things at school to help me, different pencils, the Neo, the bumpy cushion, the social worker, the occupational therapist, and the speech teacher. I have a bunch of people to help me socialize this means talk and ask questions. When people use to ask me questions and I didn't know the answers I would change the subject to things I liked to talk about. The teachers said this was confusing for people I was talking to, because we weren't talking about the same things. An example of this was someone would ask me how many weeks were in a month and I would answer "my dog likes cheese". For some reason people were confused with that response. Response is an answer to a question. I have gotten better at responses, thanks to my speech teacher. I am working with my social worker now on how to tell people not to hurt me, and to tell people what I am feeling. We play games for that, so it's not like work it's fun. My social worker is nice she tells me I can tell her anything, and I do. Mom says that everything doesn't include episodes Sponge bob cartoons. My occupational therapist is cool she helps me get over my fear of getting messy and touching gooey things. She has us carve pumpkins at Halloween and take out their guts, it's messy but she lets us wear rubber gloves if we want to, and I want to. They all let us pick prizes when we do a job well done, that's when we get the right answers or do what's call make a break through. I hope to make a lot of break throughs' so I can get more prizes.

Break Throughs'

One of my break through was when my mom, dad, and I went a big water park and I went on this rope climb. It was high and you had to walk across all these ropes like at the circus. I don't like the circus too much going on and it's loud, and scarey. I went up on the ropes, they put a harness around my waist and then attached the rope on the top rope so you could pull it with you. This keeps you from falling. I only got to the first level, I was so scared, but all night I looked at those ropes and told my mom I wanted to try in the morning. The next morning mom and I went to the ropes again, I got to the second level but not to the top. I had to stare at the ropes for a while then I tried again I got all the way to the top and down again. This is what is called break through you try and try until you can do something. I was proud of myself and so were my mom and dad, they cheered. They also told me a cost them a fortune. I think that is like money that pirates find.

Sarcasm

 My mother tells people that I have a hard time with sarcasm I don't know what that means, but she tells them the story of when my grandpa Ben saw me in my dress up clothes and said to me "what do you think that you are a princess?" I just said "thank you grandpa". She said that sarcasm would be harder for me later when I am older, I just say "okay". I love Christmas too everyone calls me a baby for believing in Santa Claus, but my mom believes in him too, so I don't feel stupid I just don't talk about it with my friends. I also like to watch Dora the Explorer sometime and Yo Gabba Gabba. Everyone says they are baby shows, but I just don't tell them anymore. Show like that help me to calm down and relax. Mom lets me watch them when homework is done to unwind. I also like to talk to kids younger than me sometimes I feel we have more in common, then friends my own age. They don't judge what I watch or what toys I like to play with like friends my own age.

My Friend Kate

Me and My friends Kate is last on right

 That's why I love my friend Kate she lets me be me and she is not embarrassed of me and we have a good time. I wish all kids with Aspbergers could have a friend like Kate she is great. Kate plays softball, and takes dance class sometimes. Dance is hard for me too many steps and I have a hard time with certain music. Slow music makes me sad, and loud music make me hold my ears. My dad is in a rock band, sometimes I listen to his band if we are outside because then it's not so loud and I can move away if it is. I like to dance to the music, but not ballet like Kate, just wiggly dances with no steps.

Things I Love to Do

I remember one time we were at Aunt Pattii's condo in Florida and we went to a restaurant they had a band playing, they were not too loud, and I got up and danced. I don't think you were suppose to dance there, but mom and Aunt Pattii let me. After a while more people came and danced it was fun. It was like swinging on the swings at the park, I like to spin on them that is what dancing is like. Dad and I like to go to the park as much as we can, I only go on the swings they are my favorite I swing high and just relax. I like the wind blowing on me, and sometimes I just lay on my belly on the swing and spin with my feet. I like to look at the ground and see what is there. When I swing high I stare at the clouds. I love to go to the park with my dad, and he doesn't care if I only swing on the swings. While we are at the park it's our turn to talk about my day, and what fun things we can plan to do soon. Dad is usually very busy working so when we get to do fun things they are the best things in the world. We go to the zoo, and the water park, and vacation. I wish we could go on vacation every week, but I have to go to school, and it's too much money. Someday I'm going to make a lot of money so I can go on vacation with my family every week. I think I'm going to be a vet or an animal scientist,

This is Dixie I rode her at Girl Scout Camp

My Pets

I love animals. I have had a lot of pets first my grandma's dog Rufus,and my dog Bob, they both died they were old and that's okay they couldn't live forever. Now I have my dog Ollie and Madilyn's ferret Tucker, oh and my goldfish glow. Ollie is crazy and likes to bite my ankles, he thinks I'm another dog. Glow doesn't do much except make the fishbowl dirty and he swims around all the time. Tucker is funny he runs sideways and hides under the couch away from Ollie. I love my pets and I help feed and take care of them so I think I should do something with animals. I cried when Rufus died because he would always wait for me when I got home from school, and one day he wasn't there it disrupted my schedule. I didn't cry when Bob died he was old and smelly, but I did love him he was gentle not like Ollie. I like to talk about Ollie a lot to everyone, my teachers, my friends, and people I don't know too well. Everybody I meet basically knows about Ollie, or my Aunt Pattii's two dogs Gordon and Pepper. We use to babysit Gordon when he was little at our house when aunt Pattii and Uncle Mike went out of town, I love him he is an Australian Sheppard, and a Blue Merle. That means he has blue skin under his fur, it's cool. He is not really from Australia, his breed is from the United States they just call him Australian I don't know why I'll have to look that up. I like to look up lots of things so I know the answers, that way I can tell everyone even people I don't know so well. People always tell me that my mom is doing a good job with me, I don't understand what that means. My mom tells me that it just means that we try a lot of things, talk about things, and keep doing things until we feel good about them. She lets me try the things I want, and she says it's okay if I don't try things that scare me or upset me. She says someday I might want to try those things, but right now we can just talk about them. She said that I have a lot of courage and that I accomplish everything on my own with just a little help from people who care about me.

My Dog Ollie

I Love to Ice Skate

It's like when I do ice skating competitions my coach Ms. Cathy helps me learn my solo and I always get a trophy, mom says so what if it's not first place you did great and you are first place with us. Then we go out for ice cream that's what I like the most. I did come in first once at Worlds competition they said that was a big deal and I was on a magazine cover for ISI, (The Ice Skating Institute), I was Alvin the Chipmunk, and I skated to the song "The Witch Doctor". My costume was red and had a big A on it. It was fun we went to Colorado and visited our friends the Manicki's. We went with our friends Kim, Arie, and Jared too. The hotel was cool and we saw lots of places, and mountains. I would like to go back there again. We went to the Stanley Hotel, it's haunted and Stephen King wrote the book "The Shining There". I haven't read it it has too many words right now and it's scarey. The movie is too scarey for me also. My favorite scarey movie is Abbott and Costello Meet Frankenstein, it's fun not really scarey and it's in black and white, I love black and white movies. My mom says it's probably because the colors are soothing to my eyes. Every Saturday my dad and I look to see what's on our favorite horror show "Svengoolie", I always hope it's Abbott and Costello Meets somebody, they are always meeting somebody. If the movies are too scarey we don't watch them. I love Saturday nights with my dad and Svengoolie.

That is me in the middle

The Starr Blades
(or the Starr Bladers like I call us)

Paying Attention

I went to see my neurologist he is a doctor that helps you with your brain. I like him he talks soft, and smiles a lot. He says that I'm so beautiful that he needs to find out what is going on in my brain. We have tried different medicines, but they would make me upset or very sleepy. Mom says I'm better off with no medicine, the doctor agrees. He said the only reason to use the medicine is to help me pay attention, but I can do that on my own with a little help. He says that school will be harder later and that maybe we should try medicine again, but mom thinks that the medicine really won't help with that. The doctor told her it's still a choice if I need it. My attention isn't always good, but mom has learned that if I am not paying attention she just yells hey little dude. I'm not a dude I tell her I am a girl, but I think she just likes saying little dude, and you know I do pay attention just to correct her. At school the teachers usually call my name a couple times, and in ice skating Ms. Cathy will hit my head with mittens and say "focus." Mittens don't hurt when they hit your head, you can't even feel them. My syncro coach Ms. Dina just yells kinda loud, sometimes it makes me want to be done skating, but just look at my friends and they aren't upset so I keep it in then it goes away. It's easier when my friends are there that way they can help me focus more because in syncro you need to focus so you don't trip anyone, or let go of the skating line. In syncro everyone is doing the same thing at the same time so I have to pay attention. Sometimes though I look up too much and Ms. Dina tells me to look straight ahead. Ms. Dina is the best synchronized ice skating coach so she has to make everyone pay close attention to things.

When I Feel Bad

  I use to have a problem looking at people in the eyes, I use to close my eyes when I talked. I don't do that as much anymore because my mom would yell "open your eyes when you talk to me, you don't have to look at me, but open your eyes." People like it when they can see your eyes, I still look up sometimes, but I'm working on it. I can look at my mom's eyes now unless I'm upset then I look up. It's hard to tell people when I'm upset, I cry with no sound so when people call my name and I don't move they pick up my head to see if I'm upset. My grandma hated that she would say it's good to cry and I should make cry noises even if they were loud. I still can't cry with sound, and I don't know if I ever will, but people who know me know when I'm upset. I don't have an emotion called anger, a lot of kids with autism do though. I use to have fits when I was younger, that is what my mom called them. I would try to hurt myself and I would yell and throw things, but now I stopped no one knows why, but I don't get angry. Mom wishes I would get angry because then people wouldn't hurt me because I could yell at them, or just scream. I don't scream I guess I don't want to hear that sound.

Bad Weather

I hate thunderstorms, the lights go out in thunderstorms. I don't want to go to school, or anywhere away from home because I'm afraid I'm going to get stuck there for a very long time. Mom says thunderstorms are cool and they are like Halloween, There is always a thunderstorm by a haunted house, but I wouldn't want to get stuck in one of those either. I know there is a scientific answer for thunderstorms, but they still start my shut down. Tornadoes are the worst I hate going into the basement for those. I like the basement I play the WII down there, but not in bad weather. Mom will put on a movie like Pooh Bear or something on the dvd player. The dish is usually not working when it's bad weather. When the power is out we light candles, mom tells me it will stop soon and to think of things like Christmas and my Christmas list. We talk about that so I don't think about the weather. I have seen the news and I know that tornadoes can take your house and stuff away so I don't ever want to see one of those. Usually during this kind of thing I'm already in shut down so I sit still or rock a little back and forth, until the weather stops.

School

At the beginning of school this year they started construction, this is where they tear down the school playground to make the school building bigger. I didn't like that they changed the school, I liked it the way it was I knew where everything was. They had to make it bigger because we had too many kids at our school and it couldn't really hold everyone. We had to make some rooms into three classroom. The teachers' needed more space, and maybe when it's done I might like it too. For now I want it back to the old way. I was afraid to that I would get stuck in the construction and they wouldn't let me go home. My mom said that she would still be there at three to pick me up and the construction wouldn't effect that. I'm always afraid of getting trapped and not being able to go home, but mom says she will always be there just like our schedule says. I have a schedule it lets me know how my day goes, it's mostly in my head except for the classroom schedule, it's on paper. Every morning my mom wakes me at 7:30 AM then I get ready for school, unless it's Wednesday then I get ready at 5:15AM we have ice skating with Ms. Cathy in the morning before school. I like to ice skate in the morning no one is really there and I can go fast. Mom and I leave for school at 8:35AM every morning, we have to be at school by 8:45AM that's when drop off is. I make sure everyday that mom know to pick me up at 3:00PM. She waits for me by the big green street light so I know when she's there. She is never late unless there is a problem. Sometime dad will get me he comes with our bicycles, or he walks. Mom and I will walk to school if my backpack is not too heavy and the weather is nice. When we walk to school I get to talk all the way, mom rather have me get all my talking out before school. When she picks me up I start again to tell her about my day that takes a while. I do my own homework, sometimes I need help and then I ask for it, but a lot of the time I do my own homework. I like to do it right after school so I can bounce on my yoga ball or roller blade. Sometimes I have a friend over and then I wait until they go home to do it.

Best Friends

After homework we talk about when we can go to visit Aunt Pattii, we don't see her as often as I like. Mom says when we go by Aunt Pattii it's only because I want to play with Kate. It's not true, I want to do both see Aunt Pattii then play with Kate. I ask everyday, mom tells me that Aunt Pattii has stuff to do most of the time. She helps out the teachers after school in a place called the ed center. She helps them clear plastic which is called laminate on their papers. She also helps them with resources, (resources are information that a teacher needs to teach a subject). They will ask for help finding websites and books. Sometimes she has parent teacher conferences, these are when your mom and dad get to talk to your teacher to see how you are doing, and what you need help with. When she has those we get to let out her dogs Pepper, she's a Border Collie, and Gordon, he's an Australian Sheppard, which I told you already, and a Blue Merle. I tell people the same information all the time in case they didn't get it the first time. I love Gordon, he is big and funny, he loves to swim in Aunt Pattii's pool. He thinks we are drowning and he jumps in to save us. He also swims in the lake in Michigan. Michigan looks like a mitten and it is north of Chicago where we live. He loves to dance with Aunt Pattii when she cleans the house.

I have a room upstairs at Aunt Pattii's it use to be my bedroom when we took care of grandma, my old toys are in it. I go up there and play when I'm over there. I like to be alone to play upstairs at Aunt Pattii's it makes me feel good to be in my old room. Aunt Pattii will always keep my stuff there so I feel safe and good, until she decides to move. Mom says when that happens Aunt Pattii will find a new safe spot for me in her new house, and she will let me pick it out. I hope she won't move ever, but when she does we will talk about it.

Aunt Pattii with Gordon and Pepper

**Things my friends and I like to do**

I like to play dress up I dress up in all of mine and Madilyn's old ice skating costumes. I also have dresses from special occasions like aunt Pattii's wedding, those are things you only wear once. Those kind of dresses are in my dress up box. My friends like to play dress up to, we put on plays, and haunted houses. Dress up is one of my favorite games, I like to pretend to be someone else. I also dress my stuffed animals in my dress up and they are characters in our plays to. I love to sing I make up my own songs, when I was little I would make up songs about what I was doing when I was singing. I don't like when people laugh so I won't tell you how my songs go. I just keep them to myself. I will sing to the radio people don't laugh at those songs. I take my singing seriously because I love to do it. My friend Jocelyn and I try to make our own web show, and on it we sing. We record our shows on my laptop and watch them ourselves. Most of the time you can't see me just Jocelyn. She sings good, but she think she is better sometimes so she sits in front of the camera. When she goes home, I make my own recording then all you can see is me and sometimes Ollie. My dad helps me sometimes since he is in a band. He is even helping me learn the guitar, it is hard for me to get my fingers on all those strings, I'm better at the drums. Uncle Mike Thompson is my dad's drummer, he lets me play his electric drums. I get to wear headphones and he makes the sound inside not so loud. Everyone says I do a great job!   That could be another thing I could be a drummer in a band, as long as they are not too loud, or play sad slow music. I think I'll stick to animals.

My Dad Singing in His Band

Other Kids with Autism

We have a friend named Frankie he has autism too, but he doesn't talk he jumps around a lot and makes noises. I watch him jump, but I can't always understand him. He tries to talk in his own way, he doesn't have Asperger's like me. I wish he could talk too, maybe some day they will help him talk so he can sing and talk about stuff with his mom. He has people who help him, and they seem to understand him. They kind of talk in special code. My mom said she watched a movie on tv about a boy who came to the United States to learn to speak, and he went to Texas (which is our biggest state, and it's in the south). They have a program there called Halo that helps kids like Frankie talk by pointing to letters and letting other people talk for them. I think that's cool, and I hope Frankie gets to do that someday.

When I grow up

My mom also told me there are a lot of people with Asperger's that go to college and get good jobs. One lady they made a movie about her name is Temple Grandin, she works with cows, she is lucky. Mom told me she makes sure that the cows don't get upset while they are at the stock yards. I will have to learn more about Temple Grandin, because I would like to go to college and work with animals like her someday. My mom says she is an inspiration to her, (this means that she sees that someone with Aspbergers can be something great), and she knows that will be me. She tells me it is already me, and that I have come along way. My dad and my mom believe in me and so do my friends and teachers. I guess we will be talking about a lot of things for the rest of my life, I can't wait.

Madi, Mom and Me